The Golden Gate Bridge
and Other Natural Wonders

The Golden Gate Bridge
and Other Natural Wonders

poems by

Han-Jae Lee

The Golden Gate Bridge and Other
  Natural Wonders
Copyright © 2013 by Han-Jae Lee
2nd printing

Book design by River Sanctuary Graphic Arts

Additional copies available from:
www.spiritualpathfinder.com

ISBN 978-1-935914-34-1
Printed in the United States of America

Library of Congress Control Number: 2013946194

All profits received by the author from sales of this book
will be donated to UNICEF

RIVER SANCTUARY PUBLISHING
P.O. Box 1561
Felton, California 95018
www.riversanctuarypublishing.com
Dedicated to the awakening of the New Earth

For my dear family

CONTENTS

I

TRAVEL

San Francisco

My friend, you will see the seashore
where the splendid blue sky
is pouring down its pails of glaring sunlight;
nearby ridges beckoning to come
on wings of fresh green foliage.

Where often chilly wind
wafts in from the Pacific;
this is San Francisco.

When you come here, my friend
you will find the Golden Gate Bridge
the pink of cherry blossoms
connecting north and south.

We could lounge on Baker Beach.
And at Fisherman's Wharf we could cook
      the entire coastline!
At the Gold Dust Lounge we'll drink and dance.

We could place our chairs facing the waves
      on the beach
and see a myriad of stars in the brilliant night sky
as we raise our eyes heavenward.

The fatigue of a long journey of flowing life behind us
we see a crowd,
a host of yellow daffodils,
fluttering and dancing alongside the beach
like the women we might meet.

Wet Fog

Wet fog comes frequently to Daly City.
Looks like fog the fine trees seem to murmur.
Wet fog blows up from the coast side of the Pacific.

Like the huge white cranes
whose wings spread throughout the city
    and one after another
suck up the parks, houses, streets, and people.

Wet fog doesn't talk all day long
and when the sunlight breaks through
returns to a far-off shore.

During its stay in the city
wet fog doesn't hurt even a petal or a dog.
Wet fog walks softly, laughing without sound,
    smiling…

Wishing to make friends with people
wet fog drops inside houses,
participates in parties and disappears.

When wet fog feels ennui it rises quickly and
    becomes the ridges of waves.
When it wishes to hear the sound of water
wet fog becomes the drizzling rain.

By the Golden Gate Bridge

After the fog lifts —a beautiful morning calm.
The broad sun comes up as usual.
The gentleness of heaven is on this bridge.

A massive structure of pink.
The bridge appears magnificent.
Wearing the beauty of the morning silently.

The blue sky is bright and glittering.

Many visitors pass over the bridge
from many countries.
Whole generations.

The travel guide to San Francisco claims:
*The earth hasn't anything to show more stately
        and beautiful*
than the Golden Gate Bridge.

Perhaps it is this brilliance that causes
an impulse to jump into the waters below.
The loveliness of the bridge tarnished
by sadness and solemnity.

Above the blue and windy sea
the sun shines on the bridge.

On the Muni Bus in San Francisco

Rush hour is always crowded on the Metro.
More passengers are standing than sitting—
not even comprehending this inconvenience.

Along the route an electric signal
continuously informs travelers of the next stop
and the next.

Some people doze like Monday morning.
Someone gurgles with a cold.
A teenage boy, wearing headphones, laughs,
    while watching his mobile phone.

It seems the passengers have deep monologues
    inwardly.
But no one converses with each other.
Only an awkward silence hangs over them.

Perhaps they understand—
like a drunkard, or a farmer, returning to his grass
    hut in the late afternoon—
that to live is to keep silent.

At intervals, an elderly grandmother
coughs with a choking sound.
The passengers avert their eyes, closing them, or
    looking out the window.

Even when a disabled old man boards
        in a wheelchair
they stand aside for him
in silence.

While the Muni bus carries this tough life slowly
I recall nostalgic moments of bygone days
and hurl a handful of tears at the window.

In moments of reverie, I miss my stop.
Firmly grasping the call line to get off.

At the Subway

At the Powell station of the BART
in San Francisco
I see an Asian man carrying a heavy bag.

He asks me the way,
pointing to the subway map with his finger.
He seems to know no English.

When he speaks with embarrassment,
    I can't understand.
It looks like he is pointing to the symbol
    for the airport.
I can tell by his body language that he worries that
    he will miss his plane.

Suddenly I recall the days
when I didn't know my way on the subway
and puzzled over what to do.

It was not easy to explain to him
with gestures and movements
that the airport train would be arriving at the
    station shortly.

I watched him
as he tried to catch the train that was going
    the wrong way.
Knowing he was not going to get
    on the airport train.

His harried actions only made things more difficult
    for him.
His fingers moved faster as he talked to
    another stranger.
Groans came out of his mouth unconsciously.

There was no one to restrain his actions;
and not only the hour of the airplane's departure
seemed to be accelerating.

At Abbotts Lagoon Beach

Here the reeds in the field are tossed about by winds.
Like an army of men in tasseled hats
    marching forward.

Swayed toward one side.
They do not behave themselves
against the winds.
They prefer to stand upright
to talk with heaven.
But winds pull them continuously
to go in their direction.

Sometimes when it is blowing a gale
    they weep loudly.
And when it rains they are filled with water.

The weather on this beach is frequently changing.
But always this salty breeze and humid air remains.
After suffering day and night, from winds
    in all directions
the heads of these reeds cannot help but hang down.

Calmly night falls here.
The whitish salt fields' panorama
spread out
beside the beach
flooded all over
with brilliant moonlight.

The Border

Monterey weather is calm and free.
Seaside aquarium crowded with visitors.
Schools of fish are swimming
inside the border.

A crowd of anchovy are dancing quickly like one
according to the fish trainer's intention.
No one is falling into disorder.

A sea otter's infant is playing ball,
sucking milk from his mother's breast.
The infant doesn't even know the visitors,
is not interested.

But mother sea otter looks anxious,
keeps a sharp lookout.
Her heart is outside in the immense blue ocean.

Inside, a lonely island!
Sealed despair.
Nostalgia's flag!

Tender affections keep hearts beating.
She misses her childhood in the vast ocean,
        her birthplace.
Never thinks of that windstorm night
when she was caught by fishermen.

In the outside border
children are chattering continually.
The youngest and the oldest are observing
inside the aquarium closely.
Infants are playing with rattles,
sucking milk from their mothers' breast.

Everybody takes great pleasure
from the inside border.
By the fish and the sea otters' sacrifice
they are enjoying.
By another's sacrifice we are taking happiness.

Inside and outside.
Ourselves and others.
The border,
Who made it?

Bronze Image of Buddha

On an open corner
at the Asian Art Museum in San Francisco,
a bronze Buddha is attentively listening, despite a
    crowd of visitors.

He doesn't care about me. Yet I approach him.
Up close I see that his ears are open to the outside:
the clamor made by men and women, the earth,
    sky, clouds, and wind...
all things in nature.

Finally, after a long time
these reverberations mingle together
and are heard simply as one sound.

The Buddha's dark-gray complexion shows me
    an eternity.
He seems to laugh at me,
enduring this waiting, endeavoring to be humble.

With eyes slightly open and grasping another's
    hand in front,
He is endlessly and eagerly listening,
seeking the noise from outside.

I close my eyes and calmly review days past.

Outside the National Cemetery

White magnolias brightly bloom
in the isolated places outside the national cemetery.

The white gravestones lined up in the cemetery
welcome the magnolias that come each year in April.

Wearing their white uniforms, the magnolias are like
    officers in the navy
receiving an inspection from their admiral.

The captivated white petals console the souls in
    the cemetery.
The souls of those who laid down their lives
    for their nation.

The souls beneath the gravestones have eagerly waited
    a long time
for their friends or relatives.

The magnolias ghostwrite the letters for the souls
    in their petals
and send them on the breeze to those who live in
    remote parts of the country.

On windy days they sing the song of April and dance
    with the branches
scattering the petals on the graves.

In the night sky interspersed with stars
the souls and petals are dreaming a dream together.

At the Unknown Soldiers' Monument

An invisible banner.
Unheard cry.
Of legendary heroes.
Obscure names.

We forgot you like a lost memory.
Enjoyed life with drinking and song
until hearing a trumpeter's requiem
on Memorial Day...

We look at the bundled flowers
before the spirits of the departed.
We pray and confess our stupidity.

You sink into oblivion while we
          consume ourselves.
Flinging our bodies into the sea of humanity,
in a fierce struggle for existence.

Your monuments are rusted with
          unfulfilled desires.
What shall we say to those
who know righteousness?

Where is the chorus of the people?
You know those who stand proudly by the flag.
You were not born for fading away.

Phoenixes!
If there is a true patriot
you are one!

Generations forget you and we are selfish.
But you are our lost conscience.
Keeper of morality until the end of time.

Highway 5

I am driving from San Diego to San Francisco.
It is midnight.
In the rearview mirror of my minivan,
trucks, wagons and sedans pass me.

A limousine with opened windows
pulls up beside me.
The driver yawns heavily.
In a pink sleeveless dress a woman leans
on the arm of a man driving a convertible.

My speedometer reads seventy-five miles an hour.
I've already gulped three glasses of iced coffee,
but still feel drowsy.
Turned up the MP3 player.
Sung a song loudly.

I stretch my lower jaw right and left with a yawn.
The GPS reveals
the distance and time
left to travel.
I pinch the flesh of my thigh.
But it is all the same, sleepy.

In a few hours I will arrive home.
If I get over this moment.
But it is not easy.

This trip is hard like the stern realities of my life.
Troubles must be passed through.
Nobody can drive my life for me.
I will plow my way along the road.

If I get over this moment
the darkness will certainly be over.
The sun will shine brilliantly.

My heart is in my home, not here on the highway.
My heart lives for the coming day.
When there is an end to passing troubles.
And delight returns.

Surfing

I am surfing today, in the middle of the
     boundless Pacific.
Surfing on the rough waves.
Though I am exposed to rain and wind everyday
I continue surfing.

Even if great waves the size of mountains arise,
I will not stop,
nor stumble,
but only manage them
to move forward.

Sometimes the waves are calm.
But at any time without notice
a huge waves tackles me,
causes me to keel over
into deep water.

Waves are my close friends,
neighbors, my life's companions;
I cannot live without them.

Sea conditions may vary from time to time,
but in order to survive life's harsh passages
I choose waves that aren't too big or too little.

I am surfing today.
I am going through the rough waves
alone.

Leave It as It Is

I see her from across the channel liner,
a nameless, uninhabited, lush island
at the bosom of the Pacific
between San Francisco and Los Angeles.

Like an inquisitive child
she is on intimate terms with nature.

The birds begin to sing before the sun rises.
Those echoes resound
and the crystal streams glide
through the valley.

Buds come into bloom.
The merry birds sing a joyous song
while the young lambs bound
under leaves so green.

What beautiful scenery there is!

Breezes pass through the leaves.
She wants to sleep by the murmuring stream.
Disturb not her dream.

Pass through her land without stopping.
Flow gently to the seashore.
Don't drop your anchor to come up.
Don't pitch a tent, don't dig a well.
Flow gently along with the shore.

Her heart leaps up when she sees
a rainbow in the sky.
She is singing a song, the winds are breathing low
and the stars are burning bright.

Flow gently by, disturb not her land.
Leave her as she is.
Leave it as it is.

New York

The city of all cities!
The city where people from every country
      live together.

At the United Nations' headquarters
you will be welcomed by the flags of all nations
flapping in the sparkling sunshine.
The flag of your homeland inspiring
      proud memories.

All the busy people!
Even so, when we struggle to find our way,
they help us kindly.
They do not lose their laughter.

When the stress of daily life accumulates
they go to Times Square
to sing and dance with friends.
Or take a break alone in midtown's Central Park.

When frustrating days greet you
look to the Statue of Liberty—icon of freedom.
She might give you wings
to fly to endless blue sky.

Thus and so, a beautiful night descends.
Numberless stars alight over the city.
Each room in the high-rise apartments is
      full of stories.

New Yorkers everywhere, like lovers that
    talk all night,
and awaken to conceive a happy dream
    the next morning.

The Umbrella

Autumn in New York's Central Park.
Rain again.

The fallen leaves once yellow, now brownish
     in color.
Scattered by the steps of visitors.

Autumn rains press the leaves to fall.

An old man sees a young couple
walking in front of him
under a partially torn
black umbrella.

The young man
holds the umbrella with one hand.
With the other
he hugs the young woman
at her waist.

Her arms entwined around his.
They are completely together.

Even though they are under the umbrella
they are soaked by the rain:
their shoulders, trousers, shoes.
Even though, they walk along humming.
Sometimes bursting into laughter.

The harder it rains
the closer they hug.
The umbrella binds them together.
A small and torn umbrella is joy enough.

Some Salesmen

David returns to Wall Street
where he and Michel sold
clothes and shoes.

They were poor and happy together then.
Driving their old Volkswagen Bus,
selling goods at a loss and at clearance.

Sometimes in the evenings they drank beer.
Disputed capitalism and business etiquette
all night long.

Once they opened a very small store
on the corner
of a back street.

Though they did their best
day and night to survive,
they finally closed it down.

Left with debt,
they scattered
each on their own.

The survival game too cold.

Now David stands in front of the banks at noon.
The buildings more magnificent and splendid
    than before.
There are many bankers in formal attire;
their faces beaming with smiles.

The small stores on the back streets are still shabby.
Many confusing signs have appeared,
but few people to read them.
Salesmen solicit them with no concern.

On the other side of the main street
hundreds of people are marching.
Demonstrating with the placard "Occupy Wall Street."
Shouting the slogan "We are the ninety-nine percent!"
    over and over.

But their slogan only scatters into the air.

Sometimes There Were Good Seasons

In a rooftop camp at the corner of Tompkins
    Square Park in Brooklyn,
on old newspapers Michael sets his fatigued
    body down.
With furrowed, unwashed face he looks down.

His comeliness gone.
His body bent and drawn over ill-fitting attire.
He gets a meal sometimes to try and care for this
    weakened form.

Once, like others, he had a wife and home.
But now he has only a feeble body
and nightmares each evening.

He tried his best to survive.
Making a livelihood,
but in vain.

After tasting life's sweetness,
now all is bitter.
Fallen into homelessness, this night he speaks.

"Michael, I am sorry.
You have always done well by me.
But what can I do?

You know that sometimes there were good seasons.
Now I cannot repay you,

even with a scrap of food or any of those
    things you need.

I think I would rather leave for asylum than
    suffer disgrace.
Then we may forsake hunger for freedom.
What do you think, my lovely body?"

Panorama of the Streets

Autumn breezes
blow the yellow leaves
off the roadside trees.
They scatter on the asphalt pavement.

A surging crowd of leaves are rambling through
      the streets
according to the winds.
They all fade to a similar color,
trampled down by shoes and tires recklessly.
My trousers brush past some of these lean leaves.

No one shows an interest in them.
Except an old woman at the bus stop
examining them carefully.
She seems to long for the vibrant colors and
      glorious times
of the past.

In the street so many people gather.
The surging crowds are moved around
here and there, according to the traffic lights.

Where do they come from? When?
How long will they be wandering from
      place to place?
Did the leaves, like them, have days of youth?

The buses come and go.
The old woman departs and others appear.
Afterward autumn leaves disappear from here.
The roadside trees will come into bud next spring.

In the night the crowds will be buried in darkness.
What is seen today is gone with the night.
Yet the panorama of the streets of New York
will remain with me for a long time to come.

The Fountain

At a Mediterranean-blue lake in Las Vegas
fountains execute an aquatic ballet
choreographed to music and lights.

Water spouts rise up together, toward space;
swinging right and left with the melody
flexibly forming circles, parabolas,
      cylindrical bottles.

Some streams play a match—
Shooting upwards continually.
Attempting to reach sky upright.

But in a moment they understand.
There is no support for them on top.
Then they come back home to emptiness.

Sometimes the fountains spray over the air,
creating a misty lake and rainbows.
Night falls, and the colors are illuminated.
Spouts and lights cross over each other
      with wild abandon.

At midnight the performance stops suddenly.
Music and lights completely covered in darkness.

On Breezy Waikiki Beach

The rainbows sing.
Sky is high through a rift in the clouds.
Too many waves to count.
Too much sand to count.
Too many days to count.

White birds skim over the sea.
Sailboards skim the calm sea.
So many colorful parasols!
Young people surfing.
Bikini-clad sunbathers.

While waves talk with sand,
rainbows, clouds, and wind,
Hawaiians drum and dance.
Like sighing for the good old days
the stories are continued with murmuring waves.

If I were wind I could hear you.

If I should meet you again after a long time,
    Waikiki,
how should I greet you?

Dream of a Marathon Runner

Marathon athletes at the starting line
in the bright sunshine
of the London 2012 Olympics.
Ready to run the course
past Buckingham Palace, St. Paul's Cathedral,
    the Tower of London.
Tagged on their front and rear with a name and an
    ID number.
After long hard years of training
they stand
as representatives
of their country.

As soon as the signal is sounded
their journey begins.
Sturdy legs propel them
toward the finish line.
They compete.
Hoping to accomplish a dream.

At the signal
some runners rush forward
to the head of the pack.
But their lead begins to shrink
after half the course is run.

The day grows hotter.

Some runners drink too much water
from the bottles offered along the way.

Some runners look often at their watches.
Only at last to give up on their journey.

Although racing brings their bodies together,
the struggle for survival is a solitary pursuit.

One runner controls his pace with precision—
suddenly surges ahead in the final stages
    of the race.
Leaping like a stag from **inside** the pack
to the front position.

Winning the race.
He becomes the gold medalist.
Draped in his country's flag.

At the finish line
the last runner to cross
tells the press,
"The journey is more important
than the medals.
Never giving up along the way,
is the final achievement."

Dreaming Each Day

What did you do today? If you ask me this,
    I did nothing.
What did you do today? If you ask again,
    I did too much.
I do something every day, but don't know exactly
    what it is.
I do nothing every day, but too busy always.

What do I gain day-to-day? I don't know.
The sun rises and the sun sets, but I don't perceive it.
There are so many stars in the sky, but I cannot
    count them,
unless I let myself fall into evening.

Waves in the ocean, sands on the beach, leaves
    in the forest,
days of our life,
How many numbers are they?
Is it utterly meaningless to talk about?

In order to know them, I'm living.

I get up every morning,
work for my livelihood, and
I cultivate myself each day.

Descartes said, *I think, therefore I am*, and they are.
From nine to five, morning to evening,
I am wasting away outwardly, but
I am renewed inwardly day by day.

Even though I am a mist that appears
for a little while and vanishes,
I don't lose heart.

For my light and momentary troubles
are ripening
a beautiful dream.

I cultivate myself each day.
I dream the dream each day.

II

LOVE AND OTHER OBJECTS
OF DESIRE

First Birthday

To an infant's bright smiles
we are playing the clown.
Laughing loud and long
at her first birthday party.

The infant keeps on laughing
as we set light to the candles.
We sing birthday songs in celebration
of this first birthday together.

Mortal life and bliss—
She doesn't know, nor does she care,
but creates pretty joy each day.
Opens blossoms, makes flowers.

Merry, merry baby!
What shall we call you?
Happiness and hope we call you.

The green field sleeps in the sun.
The small birds twitter.
The stream is flowing.

Cheerful you are, magnificent you are.
Let us keep your innocent smile long in our heart.
Think of us, lovely baby!

Can we cease to love you
when the candles are extinguished?

No, no! Surely we are with you always.
Until the end of our lives.
We love you forever!

Painting

Sometimes the carelessly lined circle
    becomes a flower.
And a casually drawn horizontal line
    becomes the place
where Earth meets up with Heaven.

I glimpse the bony branches while I sketch…
The lines on the paper become
    the morning sunlight.
Or the thorns of rose bushes.

Bright flowers bloom.

The rose thorns turn into pins which pierce the fin
of the fishes like memories
that are sleeping in the deep lake.

The lilies are shy and smiling,
hiding in the woods.

I'm listening to Vivaldi's "Four Seasons."

Outside, it is raining; gusty winds whip around me.
And lightning strikes with a loud voice.

Just at that moment the electric lights go out.
Everything vanishes into the darkness.
I light a candle and start again—

Put my pencil to the blank page.

Mummy Entreats

In a showcase of dim light
her gloomy smile captivates me.
A pale ashen-brown prehistoric mummy
lies face up on a table.
Her long black hair winds around her neck
covered in a dark green linen muffler.
Discolored teeth distorted in her open mouth.
But her face has not lost its contours, its beauty
 once perceived.

Beside her body lies a gold chain, jade earrings and
 green precious stones —
objects that indicate she was a high-ranking
 imperial princess.
Still, from the blood stains on her ragged jacket,
I suspect her last moments were tragic
and her final cries reach out to me in the silence.

When my eyes meet her eyes she pathetically
 vindicates herself.
She who was falsely accused of rebellion
 and then died.
Regardless of the explanation I read
 on the display case label
she might have been wrongly accused by rogues
 or schemers.

In the futilities of her life sometimes there were
 good seasons:

When maidservants ornamented her face and body
with jewels and perfumes...
But all vanished in a moment.
Only these articles remain as eyewitness.

Imagining the last day of the princess
I am pushed from the showcase by a
     crowd of visitors.
Though I leave the museum, her piercing cries
     follow me.

Ruby

I'm reading a book on American history.
My wife's asleep under the lamp's red-shaded glow.

On Hollywood's red carpet
Marilyn Monroe's scarlet lipstick
outlines her sunny smile.
Her cheeks are rouged too.
She arranges a red ribbon in the lapel of her jacket;
wears high-heeled shoes, the color of fire.
A crimson capped young girl presents a bouquet of
    burgundy roses.

Outside the Stars and Stripes wave in the wind.

Suddenly a shot is heard from a car in Dallas.
Blood, ruby-red, pours from President
    John F. Kennedy.
His wife, Jacqueline, cries out loudly.
Later, a single red rose is placed on the grave.

I Didn't Know That Before

I didn't know that before.
I never expected it before.
I didn't realize that you were going to leave
without saying a word.

So vain, how did you heartlessly leave
    without a sound?
Was there anything so urgent
that you could not say goodbye?

My beloved gone.

I call your name
to an empty field.
I loudly call your name out into the air.

Our firmly sworn promise
like a handful of dust
floats away in the breeze.

You appeared for a little while.
Now faded away like mist.

You'll never know I've loved you endlessly.

As you go through the years
you may repent.
Call me anytime.

Though you may look shabby,
I'll be there to wrap your broken heart.

You left, but cross-way whispers of love between us
come back
like an echo that fills a void.

Though She Left Me

Once I tried hard to escape from remembering,
but the harder I struggled, the more I was reminded.
It was no use making the effort.

We vowed not to say farewell.
I knew it was no use crying.

Though she left me,
her bright eyes, glowing cheeks and opulent lips
live in my heart.
Her sweet voice and dimpled smile
are with me too.

Memories of McDonalds, Starbucks, and
midnight movies are still with me.
The beaches of Waikiki we visited during
        summer vacation.
Central Park in autumn, trees ablaze with color.
Fallen leaves on the roadsides.
Blue sky over the snowy mountain.

The leaves are all off the trees and have traveled
        the globe.
Although our love may be buried
together with leaves,
her bright eyes, glowing cheeks and
opulent lips are still in my heart,
still alive in me.
Along with my fervent yearning.

Chopsticks

My wife and I sit together in a booth
at the bright and clean Chinese restaurant.
It is the slow hour now.

Several pairs of chopsticks are waiting
for the customers at the table.
Like troops of soldiers lined up to be inspected
they are set out in an orderly way.

A well-educated dieter, I've never hailed them.
Yet they seem to call to me...
"Hey Fatty," I hear them say.
I am anxious to be given a good name
        as a faithful servant.

Even though these chopsticks have much work to do
they have no grievance against the owner.
They always act in unison.
Not separately.

They do not discriminate by sex or race.
They form a perfectly equitable society
        of companions.

It is natural that there are keen competitions
        among men.
But imagine the gains made while cooperating
        with each other.

Prior to their work,
the chopsticks are resting for awhile together.

Retired Men's Picnic

Picnic tables on an autumn afternoon in the
    village park.
Country friends have gathered for
    a barbecue cookout.

Each has his role.
One splits the wood for kindling,
another fans the fire; roasting beef on the broiler.
Another carries the meal to the table.

A drinking bout goes on simultaneously.
Some imbibe straight whiskey,
while others drink beer from bottles and cans.

With each drink
their voices grow louder.

They chain smoke.
Revile their old bosses.
Cast aspersions on the president.

One complains about annuity insurance.
Compared to his payment
his pension is too small to live on,
his medical fees too expensive.

They repeat themselves endlessly.
There is no one to hear them.

Only the liquor bottles
look up at them
from the corners of their open mouths.

As the afternoon progresses
their tone sinks slowly
into tiredness.

Little by little
the wrinkled faces
are buried
in twilight.

Dimple

Mary was my neighbor twenty years ago,
then left for New York City.
After that I forgot her.

By chance I met her at the shopping mall.
But when she called to me I didn't recognize her.
Her face was that of a common middle-aged lady.

At first I didn't answer.

Then she called me again, "Brother!
You are the same, like a young man."
And a smile spread across her face.

Then unexpectedly,
another Mary came out
from behind the aged lady's face.
Then I remembered her dimples when she smiled.

Her two high school daughters, taller than she
broke into a chorus of dimpled laughter.
Which, until this time, they had kept,
like a flower, all to themselves.

I Am Flying

I am flying in a plane over the Pacific; it is midnight.
I sleep in a lounge chair facing upward.
My first time flying business class.
The seat is as comfortable as the billowing clouds
    outside the window.

Up until now I sat in the narrow seats of
    economy class
unable to recline fully.
The front of the plane, first class,
is a place I had never experienced.

Before I had no interest in the classes of a plane.
Going by air was enough for me;
I never thought of comparing classes.
The idea of sitting in business class was
    someone else's story.
And I didn't care about other people's
    comfortable circumstances.

There are so many passengers in the back rows
    of the plane.
Before, I didn't feel the inconvenience of the
    constricted seats.
I feel compassion for them now,
as they sleep
curled up in their narrow seats.

We are all passengers in the same outer space.
Located at around thirty thousand feet.

Our departure time and destination the same.
Flying time will be around eleven hours,
but we are segregated by classes of seats.

Before, I could perceive the comfort of business class.
But when I imagined the first class seats
my business class seat also seemed insufficient.
In order to enjoy the comfortable life, perhaps,
we must look back into the past life of poverty.

Adult School

Isabella, a working mom, with two jobs,
repeats the words in English
she is trying to memorize.

Before her eyes they seem to escape.
As soon as a word enters her right ear
it vanishes from her left.

Before she completes a page in her textbook
she forgets the contents of the first line.
Her second daughter's crying face appears
    in her memory.
The daughter who has caught a cold, again.

Isabella works at the laundry, part-time
    weekday afternoons;
at a fine restaurant in the evenings.
But she is dreaming of becoming a police officer.

Her classmate Daniel is an auto mechanic.
He is looking for words
in the dictionary
while listening to the teacher's lecture.

An old man who is retired writes words on a page.
He'd like to write his memoir in English.

Fifty students, whose motherland and races
    are different,
share their enthusiasm for revealing that their
    difficulties are the same.

Dozing

I wake to the sound of a waterfall—
a cruise over invisible Buffalo Falls;
I hear a burst of applause.

I notice a pool of saliva on my tan jacket;
Wipe it up.
Try not to doze off again.

To chase off my drowsiness
I hit my thigh, clear my throat, rub my eyes;
Certainly not! I will not fall asleep again!

I admonish myself.
Tilt my head to concentrate.
Absorb the lecture on philosophy.

After awhile I wake
to the noise of a crashing waterfall again.
But there is no water.

Only the din of applause
in the full conference room.

I ask myself: *Isn't this strange?*
I've never napped before
while listening to a teacher's lecture.

In this somnolent condition
I see myself now, trying to awaken.
But all self-persuasion is in vain.

As soon as I let myself off the hook
I plunge into Buffalo Falls again.
Startled by laughter as I shout for help.

The Last Day of the Year at the Neighborhood Coffee Shop

The coffee shop near Penn Station in
    New York City
is always crowded with customers.
Patrons craving mochas and lattes.

Plastic white chairs arranged beside tables
positioned differently and frequently
by hard-working employees.

The workers' bodies, all skin and bones;
as they work they make no sound—
perhaps their voices and bodies are shrunken by
    the recent bitter cold.

Their weak legs seem ready to collapse from a long
    day's work.
Like tired beasts of burden;
They do not bark at strangers; nor creep up
    on them.

Instead, meek as working cattle
they serve others over a lifetime.
Without reward.

They might not have received an education before
    arriving in New York.
That's why they have no complaints.
Instead they offer comfort with a humble mind.

While I see the old year out and the new year in,
the last day of the year, I quietly review
    my conduct;
And remind myself to do more for others.

Imprisoned Words

Impatient and perplexed,
persistently scratching the floor with her claws.

Her large eyes
seem to speak
something urgent and painful.

But I have no ears to hear it.

All her requests to me, everything she wants,
seems to be in her eyes.
The words held back like tears that don't spill out.

Words that can find no way to come.

Even though she is making an appeal
still there is no sound; still the words
do not budge.

What I can do?
Only pass my hand over her head repeatedly.
Make a trip to a veterinarian.

Who can open the prison
that has confined these words
for millions of years?

You Are Mine

Every Wednesday Mrs. Brown frequents the
   grooming salon at PetSmart.
Though she makes an appointment, the salon is
   always busy.

She takes her poodle, Eddy for a haircut.
Sometimes a bath, blow dry, and brush.
Nails manicured, polished, trimmed, all included
   in the price of the service.
For a healthy smile, she cleans Eddy's teeth at
   home every day.
Bathes Eddy with her shampoo, dries his body;
massages his coat with a mixture of jojoba oil,
   chamomile and aloe for a light finish.
She puts a pink ribbon in Eddy's hair, red shoes
   on his paws.

When she goes out she always puts shoes
   on the poodle—
in spite of Eddy's groans.
She puts a striped jacket on Eddy's back
even in sultry weather.
On sunny days she puts sunglasses on Eddy.
All his accessories are changed according to her
   desires, not Eddy's.

Mrs. Brown had a veterinarian cut Eddy's tail for a
   beauty show.
She almost had the vet cut off part of his ears!

She never thinks about Eddy's feelings at all.
She believes that Eddy belongs to her.
And doesn't think about the animate creature.

When a rainy day comes
Eddy turns round and round repeatedly.
Seeking a trace of his tail.

Hamlet Park Afternoon

Five-o-clock in the afternoon:
A village whose people love dogs.

Every afternoon big dogs out taking a walk
    with their people.
Sometimes the dogs and their masters
    just ahead of me...

Dogs let loose in a patch of grass.
Dogs move their bowels once free.

A Bulldog barks at a Greyhound for some reason.
A small mongrel wags its tail, sniffing
    another dog's anus.

A maiden embracing a poodle
enters the park.
Teenagers shouting to a Shepherd,
tossing a Frisbee to train him.

A middle-aged man in a blue beret
walks five dogs
past the children's playground.
The dragon tattoo on his forearm
bulging as he tries to restrain them.

A gray-haired couple
arrives at the entrance.
Disappointment and fear on their faces—
so many dogs!

66

A young woman pushes a baby carriage,
walking gingerly with her Boxer.

The sun sets behind the western mountains.
And the round full moon rises in the east.

Renaissance Woman

The *Seoul Supermarket* is always crowded.
The owner, Mrs. Kim greets customers with a "Hi."
Shaking hands and all the time smiling a
    toothy smile.

People prefer to call the market *Hi Super.*

Mrs. Kim is known as a renaissance woman.
Especially knowledgeable about the customs
    of Asian countries
and daily life in America. Mrs. Kim speaks
    fluent English.

Her husband, John, also greets every customer
    with "Hi."
They impart a generosity to Asian, European and
    African-Americans alike.
They do not forget to create a feast for them.
The customers are like close friends of the Kim's.

Yet, when friends ask to celebrate the Kim's
    wedding anniversary,
Mrs. Kim doesn't even know the date or the year of
    the marriage.

Puberty

The weather is fine today
but yesterday was windy with rain.
The day before yesterday was also stormy.

Due to recent unexpected changes
it is not possible to forecast what the weather
    will be.

Today Emily didn't go to school;
and she didn't eat anything.
The day before yesterday she didn't go either,
but that was because of the rain.

Lately she received high scores in mathematics
but still was not happy. Sometimes she
convulses with laughter in her room or
whimpers without reason.

Sensitive to every little whisper
she responds with a scream.

Stifling his emotions, Emily's father firmly kicks
a rugby ball around the playground.
Uncertain where it will land.

A Living History of Sports and Entertainment

I'm going to dump my sports shoes in the trash.
Shoes which have been my faithful companions,
trainers and close friends for the last five years.

Though we didn't agree on much at first,
gradually we made concessions to each other.

Sometimes these shoes led me to the tennis court in
      the early morning
or took me to the playground for exercise.
I often trained hard in these shoes.

But on weekends and holidays they guided me to the
      perfect spot for a picnic
or to the mall for shopping.

When I fell ill they took me to the theater
to experience a living history of sports and
      entertainment.

Over time I felt these shoes
causing a strange imbalance in my body.

I discovered the bottom soles were worn irregularly.
Perhaps it was time for me to leave them.

It is regretful, but I had to abandon them.
Is there anything that does not grow old
     in this world?

Filing Cabinet

A rusty filing cabinet stands in the corner
    of my office.
The painting worn off, discolored.
The door is loosened, the doorknob twisted.
I have used it for more than twenty years,
even as a young businessman.

When she first came to my office
this model was new,
smart, and very smooth
each time I opened the door.
I was the only man to open her.

Nobody knew
the combination, but me.
I trusted the cabinet
with all kinds
of valuable documents.

Every day I opened and
closed it
repeatedly.

Sometimes I slept
in the office
all night with it.

I took my food and coffee
with the cabinet
nearby.

With my expanding business
other filing cabinets came into the office.
They were more colorful, fashionable
with modern functions and safety devices.

These new features —
so convenient and useful.

The battered cabinet became a place
merely for storing old documents.

Years later I forgot the combination.
I tried many times to open the drawers, to no avail.

It felt like rock. The door stayed firmly closed.
Until it was forced opened by a locksmith.

The Black Stone Mermaid: Is Life the Dream of Dreams?

There was a virgin, pure of heart, who was planning to marry a young man who worked on the newly formed crew of the RMS Titanic. The ship was on its maiden voyage, traveling from England to New York.

The port was clear as glass.
So smooth it was calm.
Truly that hour never had a sinister feeling
when he departed for New York.
The biggest ship ever built was cheered.
Merrily voyaged on her maiden journey.

Is life the dream of dreams?

But all dreams had vanished into the deep sea
as pieces of the ship crumbled.
Pieces of fantastic times.
Ecstatic days.

Yearning to lose herself in unattainable love
she didn't believe the news.
Couldn't believe in it.
Never admitted it.

"Fiancé never die, we are dreaming only.
The dream will be over very soon."

Is life the dream of dreams?

Though love has gone
memories remain.
Love stories don't fade.
She strongly held that
her fiancé would be coming back soon.
Of course.
Must be coming back. No doubt in her mind.
"Where is your vow? Give me back my heart."

What is the yearning?
Is it a mist that appears for a little while
then just fades away?
Is it the dream of dreams for a moment?

From morning till evening.
Day to day.
Each month,
every year
of her life.

She sits at the beach
scans the horizon.
Waits for her fiancé.
Calls his name repeatedly.
No longer eats or sleeps.

Still there is no answer,
"Give me back my love, my heart!"

In silence and tears.
In silence and tears.

This yearning for unattainable love
burnt her heart.
The lovely body grew dark and blackened.

Sometime later she became a black stone.
Resembled a mermaid.
Left the world.

What is the yearning?
Is it a mist that appears for a little while
then vanishes like smoke?

Is life the dream of dreams?

III

SEASONS

Welcome Spring

You, my lover of spring, who has returned to me.
Please give me the chance to embrace you again.
For I am penitent after my foolishness.

Yearning like an orphan who has lost her parents.
Hugging my heart.
My lover of spring.

Please help me recover the burning passion
that has cooled in your absence.
Let your warm smile sprout blossoms that have
    withered away.

You, my lover of spring,
I never groaned or complained of any discomfort
while I waited for you.

Let's enjoy a picnic under the cherry blossoms.
Let's sing in chorus.
Welcome spring!

You, my lover of spring, who has come back again.
Let's go together and not separate again.

Whispers of Spring

I open the window suddenly,
believing I hear
last year's fallen leaves
rustling in the wind.
But they are not there.

Instead, I hear whispers
from the yellow sprouts
of forsythia in the garden.
Buds just forming
from thin branches.
Perhaps the yellow color of buds
call and halt me.

In the park I see branches of white magnolias
        in full bloom,
red azaleas and pink cherry blossoms
moving in the breeze.
Their flowers come early,
before their leaves.

Messengers of the season, they knock.
First to awaken spring!
Bringing the light of the sun.
Causing the streams to flow.
Singing a song that twittering birds join.
Forcefully launching a fresh spring.

These messengers tell me that spring has come.
But will vanish without much notice.

Cherry Blossoms

During the cherry blossom festival
pale pink flowers cover the entire sky.

Laughing and waving their hands
they gladly greet me.

Their sunny smiles and fresh smells
wash away the fatigue of daily life.

It's like a beauty contest
with musical instruments in a schoolgirls' band.

The flowers are singing songs all along
and even dancing in the breeze.

With all the flowers so similar
how do I choose the most beautiful?

Looking more closely, I see that, like the faces
    of people,
the countenances of the flowers are different.

Similarly, we may be seen as the same person
    by the flowers.
They have their own universe; embrace sunshine,
    dew, wind and sky as they blossom individually.

How long will the festival of ecstasy continue?
Can they know the way to eternal joy?

Desires toward what is beautiful
may lead us endlessly.

Toward the End of Cherry Picking Season

Monday morning
after a weekend full of pickers.
Toward the end of cherry picking season.

All the lovely guests had come together
like the inflow of tides.

Taking joyfully the fresh and virgin cherries.
Until fully satisfied.

Now gone as tide ebbs.
Only a few cherries
hang lonely on the trees.

In order to be loved
the cherries waited a long time.
Together with the farmer from the beginning
     of spring.

The sky darkened with clouds and
peals of thunder were heard frequently.
The cherries brightened their bodies
with deep red lipstick.

The harmony of the cherries' colors and their dreams
at last fulfilled
by those who picked them.

Watermelon

She relaxes with a smile.
In joy and sorrow she welcomes all people
with looks of delight.

Her disposition is that of a good-natured person.
Though her external features have
    well-rounded corners
her heart is filled with sharp passions.

Her nature is to help others.
She gives willingly of herself
to those who are thirsty.

Reminds them not to swallow
the seeds,
while taking her flesh.

Morning Glory

Turning the corner in front of my house
a purple morning glory seems to beckon.
But I can't stop for her
or I'll be late for work again.

Even though I can see through the gaps
    in the fence
that she is blooming brightly
in the morning sunlight and dewy grasses
I cannot stop now.

She looks unwilling though to have me take leave.
Even bows down to me in the breeze.
I thought I would have time to love her
when I returned later.

However, she did not wait for me.

Though she had looked so gorgeous earlier
by the time I went back
in late afternoon
she had faded.

Dandelion

One yellow dandelion blooms
alone by the fence.
On the other side
people are busily coming and going.

The dandelion flower seems to have much curiosity
    about these people
and tries to lean toward the pedestrians.

But the dandelion leaf worries that someone will
    tread on the flower.
The leaf makes an effort to hold the petals back, so
    they do not lean.

The fence also exerts pressure on the flower—
holding her back.

The breeze blows over in the leaf's direction
trying to help the leaf stall the dandelion's progress.

Spring noon's sunshine falls in snatches
    around the pedestrians
creating power for the leaf through photosynthesis.

The dandelion, smaller than the other flowers,
is perhaps curious about tall things.

Eventually this curiosity turned into spores and
    dispersed in the air.
Then white dandelion seeds wandered away
    riding the wind
flying away to the end of the sky.

For the Chrysanthemum

When other flowers fall in autumn
she blooms alone.

Despite frosty mornings,
her work is to become glorious petals.
And the air is laden with the scent
    of chrysanthemums.

In order to come into bloom
the chrysanthemum endures
scorching heat that confines her for days
    in summer.

She hears rolls of thunder in the distance
and feels heavy showers falling whole days.

She sees flocks of swans fly away through dark
    clouds before sunset.
She is cultivated from gentle breezes
    in the mountains.

In her short life, the chrysanthemum has
    experienced prosperity and adversity.
Once the chrysanthemums are fallen,
    no other flowers remain.

I pray to God, I wish not to follow her too soon
into the dark and cold winter night.

Unknown Flowers in the Valley

The flowers bloom.
The flowers bloom.
The unknown flowers bloom
in the valleys of the mountain
from spring to summer.

Because of loving the silence,
the flowers bloom alone.
The flowers bloom lonely
among the weeds
in the secluded valleys.

Because of loving the sun,
the flowers bloom from day to day.
The unknown flowers bloom
from day to day continually.

Because of not wanting
to show their shabby leaves,
the flowers fade away in the evening.
The flowers fade away together with the wind.
The unknown flowers vanish away silently.

While Sweeping the Leaves in My Back Yard

In autumn I sweep the leaves every day.
There are many kinds of deciduous trees
older than neighboring evergreens.

In spring, these trees come into leaf
        at different times,
but descend in autumn simultaneously
after the color has faded.

In summer, the leaves grow luxuriantly
taking various shapes that cast shadows
that block the glaring sunlight at noon
and call up mysterious forest spirits and creatures
on a windy evening.

In frosty autumn, once upright and
        prosperous leaves
hang their browning heads down.
The fallen leaves lie down together in the recesses,
        living together peacefully.

I sweep the leaves together.
Assembling them into piles outside my yard.
To be taken away by the garbage truck
        in the morning.

Growth Ring

In the front yard of my house
stand several large maples.
Taller than all the others
in the neighborhood.

As soon as they appear ready to bud in spring
I take notice.
Watch intently each day as the leaves
        grow luxuriantly.
Finally forming a dense, gloomy thicket in summer.

My windows look out into the garden, and
even though I take tea every day
seeing the same trees outside
I do not anticipate them turning with autumn's color.

Many squirrels live in these trees.
Spending their time scurrying up and down.
Once one, while going down, suddenly stopped
to look at me, his eyes meeting mine.

After a meal in the dining room
I climb the stairs to my second floor study,
and a squirrel also goes up to the top,
by way of the trunk of the tree.

The maple leaves, now brown, have fallen.
In such a short time the trees have become scrawny.

When evening falls all things
are covered with darkness.
Another morning is preparing to be opened.
Each day is just like every other day.

The squirrels and I travel up and down
and the tree's growth ring increases annually.

The Last Leaf of Autumn

All, all are left but one;
the last lonely leaf swaying in cold winds.

Showing her silvery underside;
destined to come down soon.

All her lovely companions
have faded away.

The branches of the trees are thin—
their leaves all vanished.

Hour by hour it grows colder.
Just before sunset the clouds drop down.

Like the leaf,
I almost fall fluttering in the wind.

Like the leaf, I nearly fall fluttering
from the branches of myself.

In days past I missed out on something spiritual.
And I wasted time and effort.

If I were a balmy breeze I'd talk with her.
If I were a swift cloud I'd fly to former days.

I will not leave her to waste on the branch.
All will join me in singing her praises.

Ripened Pumpkin

Loose and abundant woman.
Woman of lenient mind
lying on the sofa.

She offers comfort
and humor
I rest in her sunny smile.

Innocent, round, nude.
Fattened from soil
and earth.

The Heavy Snow, The Chaos

I

All day, every day, the snow is falling ceaselessly;
Until all things on the earth are covered with snow.
And due to severe
descending
snow
visibility is nearly zero.
It seems that a piece of the heavens has quietly
        opened,
failing to control the quantities of snow falling to
        earth.
Or perhaps after being scolded by the heavens
the clouds work off their vexations with
        heavy snowfall...
Like a master kicking a dog who has disobeyed.

II

At the first snow day, the yards and roads were
        slightly covered
with light and soft snowflakes.
Everything was rounded off, smoothed over,
        magnificently.
However, the next day, the true character of the
        snowflakes was revealed.
Then they submerged the alleys and cars nearly
        to their windows,

broke the trees and roofs of barns.
Piled up snow closed the doors of houses
    and stores.
Now confines all citizens to their homes.
The city was put out of commission by the snow.

III

The snow, although trampled and humbled,
still behaves perversely.

One Freezing Day

Minus twenty-one degrees Celsius this morning—
The mountains, rivers, lakes, trees, and even
    myself, are frozen over.

In freezing days such as these
I imagine
descending
into the earth
and living there
together
with roots.

And even though the earth is frozen with ice
and all the grasses are withered,
I will hear the murmuring
of the brooks that flow
through the numerous roots in the ground.
Underground tubers and bulbs preparing
for new life
with the coming spring.

And in the ground beneath
I may be invited by the moles to a
    New Year's Eve party.
Where warm in their burrow perhaps I will see
    their folk dances
that I never experienced above ground …
What genial places there are underground!

I imagine
after the winter season passes
I will return home,
together with the frogs.

The Day Is Snowing, I'm Comfortably Warm

All morning
slow clouds smoothly flying
over the front
and back yard.

For the last several days
low clouds hanging
in the foreground of the mountains.
Covered with a veil of clouds.

Day and night whole clouds
assemble in the Heavens.
Preparing great snowflakes.
Now falling softly and silently through the bare
    branches of trees.

It's as if someone operates a magnificent factory
    in the sky.
Where all kinds of clouds, long shreds and
    tatters of fog,
the cries of birds, and even the sound of words,
are mixed.

And stripped of color, become
these snowflakes descending to the fields.
Like green sugar cane changed
to white refined sugar in the factories.

The day is snowing, I'm comfortably warm.
Even though the weather is below freezing.
I walk up and down through the hamlet park
humming "White Christmas."

Great snowflakes are falling in the pines.
Making big snowy tassels in the boughs.

From above, the clouds are gazing on the
        astonishing panorama of our hamlet.
From the clouds, the snowflakes are descending
        continuously.

And my buoyant mind is ascending to the sky
like a balloon.

A Snowman Smiled

In the calm and emptiness of the hamlet park
a sturdy lad stands alone in front of a tall pine.
He is a horrid and ridiculous figure.

His left arm is broken.
One large eye made with charcoal and deep-black
    eyebrows almost gone.
A mustache made with pine needles is cut in half.
Only traces of a nose and mouth remain.

In his right hand he tightly holds
    an American flag,
like a soldier wounded in many battles.

I feel pity for him.

I restore his arm, eyes, eyebrows, mustache,
    nose and mouth.
Then after reinforcing the face and body
    with snowflakes,
I cover his neck with a red muffler.

I think he will be happy and smile at last.
But still he looks wooden, expressionless, lonely.
So I make another snowman exactly the same
    beside him.

And as I turn to head toward home
I hear a deep laughing voice at my back.

Into The Snowy Field

When he entered the university from Korea
he had no spare clothes.
Wearing dark blue jeans the first day,
and every day, until he graduated.

His classmates thought he had an obsession
    for jeans.
But he confided in me
that once in a while he would have liked to have
    worn leather pants,
a jacket with a fur lining.

After we spoke
he walked across the campus
into the field
toward the horizon
with big flakes of snow falling
as they had for several days.

After graduation we scattered.
Each to survive on our own,
out in the vast field of the world.

I saw his portrait in the paper,
set out with a border of white chrysanthemums.
I read about the car accident on the highway
    during a snowy winter day.

In the photo, he was wearing blue jeans.
Who else but I knew?
How he wished to wear the warmth of leather
in cold weather.

Fish Sleep

The fish in the Chinese supermarket stare up
    at the customers.
While the salesman touts their stellar attributes,
    fish eyes glare.

The fish on the grill stare up at the cook.
Out of the burning fire their eyes glower.

Like singers their mouths are fully opened,
but without the blinking eyes of chorus members.

When they were caught by the fisherman's
    casting net
they strongly refused; opening their mouth to feed
    one last time.
As the air tightened around the fish gills…as death
    approached finally.

The fire burns the fish, eyes still wide open.
Eyes that have no eyelids.
Eyes that neither sleep nor death can close.

When fish sleep the wide Pacific lays a blanket
    over them.
The sea sings a lullaby to sleep.

While the fish burn on the grill, no one listens.
But the fish mouths are still wide open.

As if they had all joined in singing
the blue waves of the sea.

Ice Trout Fishing

There is a tense moment
felt between what's above the ice and what's below.
Only the fishing line serves as an intermediary.

Dim and far from man's reach,
in the deep part of the lake where trout live.
Where hunger stares him in the face.

While keeping quiet beneath thick ice;
always anxious about news on the surface.
What goes on there?

In a slight tent the fisherman spends three days.
Bores a small hole through the ice.
Drops the fishing line with night crawlers on an
        angler's hook.
Still no biting signal.

Below,
the trout keep their full attention on the delicious
        smelling bait.
Ecstasy and uncertainty— their appetite, leading
        them into temptation.

Above,
strong cold ennui for the fisherman.
A parallel tension between trout and man.

View of the Thawing

Thawing snow runny like rice gruel.
As the poor city streets
regain their original appearance.

Boarded up houses, decrepit from lack of care,
    show their fatigue.
The leaking roofs repaired with plastic sheets
to protect them from relentless rain.

Sidewalks, forcibly awakened from slumber,
now exposed to a medley of noises from cars,
    children, loudspeakers.
Sidewalks, previously embedded in snow, revealed.
Heaped with trash and dogs' dung,
    miscellaneous fluids…

The face of the city, fair-skinned, like an
    imperial princess.
Thawing, slushy, soppy.
Her snowy makeup rapidly effaced by
    a spring breeze.

Glasses In Winter

It is minus degrees and cloudy.
It feels like it could snow.

The bus stop at the early commuter hour is teeming
with the salaried workers standing in line.
Waiting—I am one of them.

I get on the Number 7 bus, as I do every morning.
But suddenly my view is blocked entirely.

I flounder at the threshold.
Then, like a blind man
stumble to find a seat.

But there is no way to see.
Until the vapor curtain from the outside
    is drawn back.

I never expected this invisible enemy.
Hiding in the air, attacking my glasses.
Over the wide differences of temperature
    and humidity.

Mountain in the Foreground

The mountain in the foreground of my village
    forecasts the weather.
In the morning I see the mountain's features
    from my bed.
Sunny days are a short distance away.

Sometimes dark clouds move across the mountain,
linger for a while on the ridge, then disappear
suddenly.

On other days gigantic cumulus clouds
hang on its peak like a huge balloon.

In rainy season the mountain is covered with
    clouds, the mountain invisible for days.
Heavy clouds rush across the ridgeline and
    showers follow.

Sometimes the fog covers the forest
spreads her skirt all the way to the village.

In the evening the sky over the mountain
shows a halo round the moon.
And then I forecast it will rain tomorrow.

The mountain changes his clothes every season.
Sometimes it is green;
after that the hills are aflame with autumnal hues.
Even when I do not notice.

The mountain ridge is the gate of the sun, the
    moon and the birds.
Flocks of swans fly away just before sunset—
Orange in a sky full of purple feathers.
Before the winter snowcaps appear on top
    of the hill.

After Darkness

There is no life that has not experienced the
    darkness of midnight.
All kinds of resilient flowers bloom in the world.
After surviving both day and night they offer sweet
    scents to passersby.

There is no flower that has not experienced
    the wind.
All kinds of magnificent flowers bloom
    in the world.
While their stems are tossed about in the wind,
    once stilled they stand straight.

There is no flower that blooms without getting wet
    from rain.
Moisture like tears, sends nourishment to roots.
Stronger they grow, larger, more vivid.

In spite of wind, rain, time of day, many flowers
    have bloomed.
All kinds of fruit have been born.

Is there any life that has not experienced
    ups-and-downs?
Is there any love that has not gone through
    highs and lows?

Seeking a Secluded Life

Sometimes I wish to live in seclusion:
In a deep valley where there is no telephone,
no television, no computer.
No incoming news ... only the sounds
of sparrows and mountain streams.

Sometimes while sitting on a tree branch
    or a boulder,
dipping my feet in a stream,
I quietly recall past days.
Yet surveying all I have toiled to achieve
everything seems meaningless.

Once I followed after rainbows,
chased after the wind.
But I don't want to struggle to exist anymore.
I hope to fully enjoy a life of seclusion
with nature as my neighbor.

If I miss my friends in the valley,
I will go down to the post office and send a letter;
then return to my nest in a leisurely way—
where I will sing together with unidentified birds
and play a game of hide-and-seek
with the fawns in the forest.

Handwritten Letter

I wrote a handwritten letter to a dear old friend
who lives in the rural village of my homeland.

Over the past several years, I have sent
      only e-mails,
so now handwriting feels unfamiliar to me.

I place the letter in an envelope;
try to write his name and address on it.

At that moment, mountain brooks flow
      from my pen;
sparrows fly up and I hear the songs of the birds.

My study becomes the orchard hut; the farmland
      covered in green,
apricot pink blooms, plum blossoms, ripe cherries
      and apples.

In the heat of summer, the sound of thunder and
      bolts of lightning come;
In the fall, farmers store up grains in the barns
      for later.

Snowy winter comes, then
spring follows.

Even as the seasons change repeatedly,
our friendship is deepened.

I remove the letter from the envelope
and add a lyric he likes to the last line.

At the post office I quietly recall his name again,
and drop the letter into the mailbox.

My Father Is With Me

My father passed away a long time ago.
But he is still with me.
He never went to school.
But knew everything.
He knew what love was.

I loved my father like he loved me.
He was neither rich nor proud.
Never said to do good.
But did good works always.

My father knew the way to fix trust.
And keep it.
He knew the right way to sail through
     life's journey.

When I went astray in my life
he told me, "There is nothing you cannot do."

My father was not a doctor,
but he healed the sickness of my body and mind.
When I grew weak,
he trained and disciplined me.

My father has passed away.
But he is in my heart as a master compass.
My soul is always steeped in joy with him.
In his breast I sleep,
dreaming in the sound

his breathing kept,
and in the surging crowd,
toiling, striving from day to day.

Knowing whatever happens,
my father is with me.

HAN-JAE LEE began writing poetry in 1997. He studied poetry and creative writing at Chung-Ang University and Korea University in Korea, and also in the United States, attending writing workshops at the Aptos and Campbell Public Libraries and at the Almaden Community Center in San Jose. In 2005 he won a poetry award (silver) in a national poetry contest for his work, *A High-rise Apartment*, given annually for an outstanding poem, sponsored by The National Assembly of Korea and The Federation of Korean Cultural Center. His first poetry collection, *A High-Rise Apartment*, was published in Korea in 2008. He also co-published three poetry anthologies and his poems have appeared in the magazines, *Literary Movement and Trend*, *Literature World* and *Vision of Poetry* (all in Korean). He has been writing poetry in English since 2004 and this poetry collection is his first book in English. He lives in both San Jose and Seoul.

www.ingramcontent.com/pod-product-compliance
Lightning Source LLC
Chambersburg PA
CBHW031517040426
42445CB00009B/265